Library of Congress Cataloging-in-Publication Data

Arnosky, Jim.
All about alligators / Jim Arnosky. p. cm.
ISBN 0-590-46788-3
1. Alligators — Juvenile literature. [1. Alligators.] I. Title.
QL666.C925A76 1994 597.98 — dc20 93-41045 CIP

12 11 10 9 8 7 6 5 4 3 2 1   4 5 6 7 8 9/9

Printed in the U.S.A.   37

First printing, September 1994

The artwork for this book was painted in watercolor.

Book design by Kristina Iulo

ALL ABOUT
ALLIGATORS

Jim Arnosky

 Scholastic Inc. New York

This book is dedicated to
Sid and Kathy.

Have you ever wondered about alligators?
Where they live?
What they eat?
How big they grow?
Are they dangerous to people?

This book answers all
these questions and more.
It is all about alligators!

Alligators, turtles, snakes, and lizards are reptiles. Reptiles are cold-blooded animals. "Cold-blooded" means that these animals control their body temperature not from within, as we do, but by moving to a warmer or cooler place.

A small alligator shares a warm place with its three modern reptile relatives.

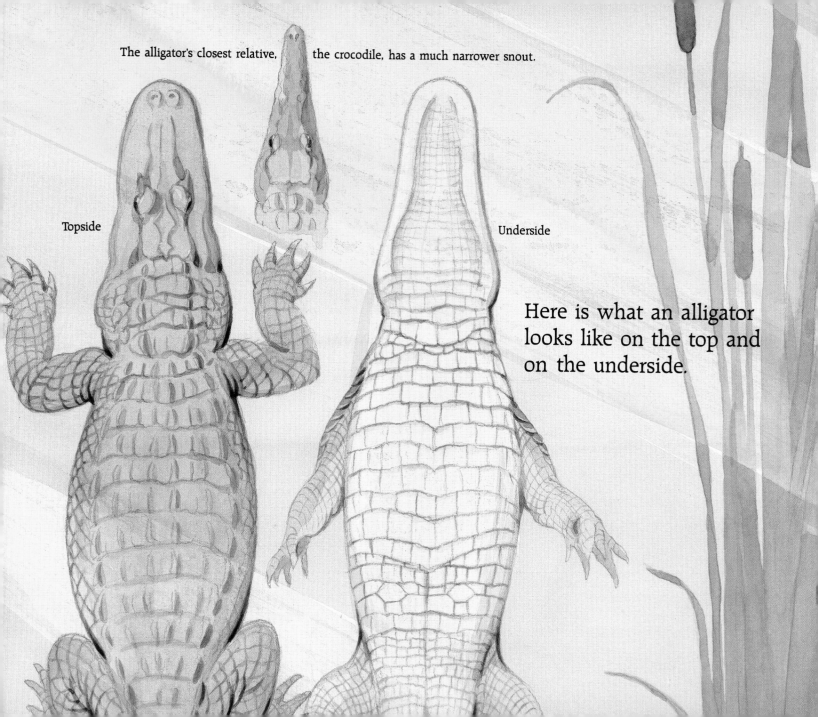

The alligator's closest relative, the crocodile, has a much narrower snout.

Topside

Underside

Here is what an alligator looks like on the top and on the underside.

Alligators have a third eyelid, which is transparent for seeing underwater.

An alligator's ears are hidden inside flaps of skin behind the eyes.

Alligators have huge, powerful jaws for grasping prey — animals that are hunted and eaten by other animals.

All of an alligator's teeth are sharply pointed for holding on to prey.

Alligators can be either green, blue-gray, or black in color.

United States

The watery realm of
the American alligator

Actual size of an
alligator hatchling

Alligators are semi-aquatic, which means
they spend nearly half their time in water.
Alligators inhabit rivers, lakes, canals,
marshes, swamps, and bayous.

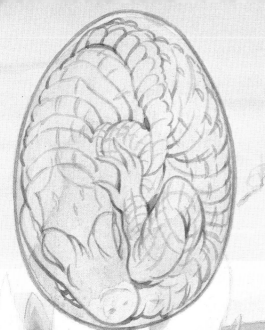

A female alligator may bury as many as 60 eggs in her nest of mounded-up grass, leaves, and mud.

Alligator eggs are hatched by the heat of the sun. The eggs hatch in nine weeks.

This is the actual size of an alligator egg, with a peek at how a 10-inch alligator might fit inside.

Mother alligators watch over their young for as long as two years. They are fierce protectors. Never approach a baby alligator, even if it appears to be abandoned. Its mother will surely be somewhere close by.

1 year = 2 feet long

3 years = 4 feet long

5 years = 6 feet long

After five years, most of an alligator's yellow tail markings have faded away.

American alligators grow about one foot in length each year for their first five years. After that they grow more slowly. Alligators can live 50–60 years and can grow to almost twenty feet long!

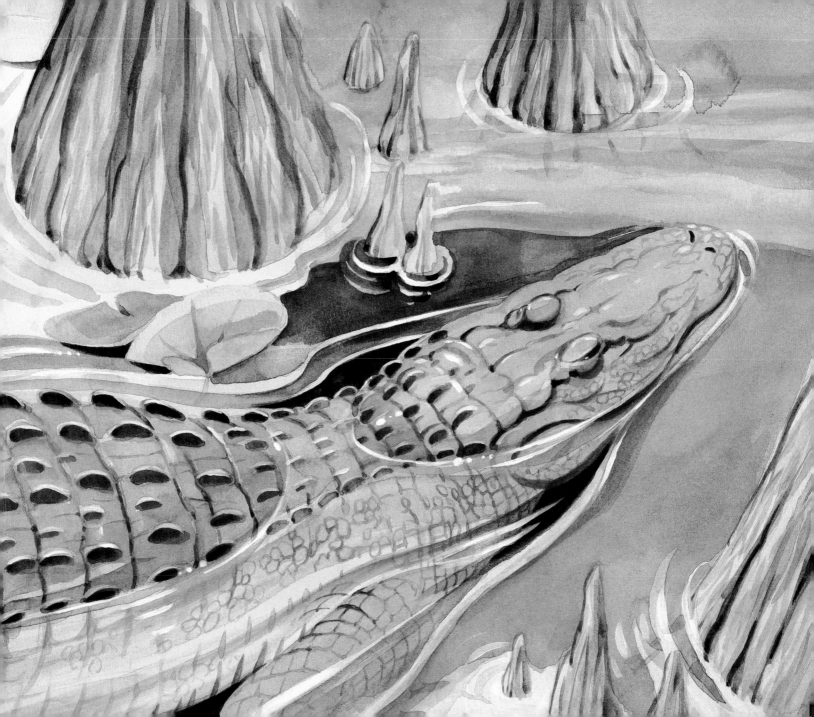

If alligators are aggravated, they will either grumble or roar. When threatened, they hiss. During mating season, male alligators produce a deep throaty bellow, which attracts female alligators.

Baby alligators have their own special sound of alarm. A baby alligator's repeated call of "YeeOck!, YeeOck!" quickly brings a mother alligator to the rescue.

Alligators will eat any animal they can catch. Insects, fish, softshell turtles, water snakes, wading birds, muskrats, raccoons, and otters are all regularly eaten by alligators.

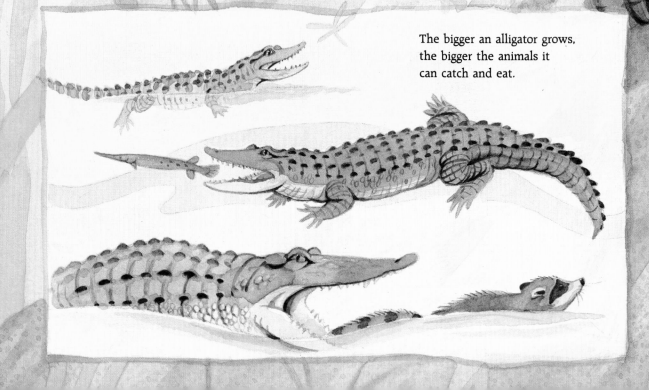

The bigger an alligator grows, the bigger the animals it can catch and eat.

When an alligator's belly is full, the alligator becomes very lazy. It may not hunt again for days.

When stalking prey, an alligator swims with most of its body submerged. Only its eyes, and sometimes its nostrils, are above the water. The victim is unaware that it is being stalked until the alligator strikes.

See how an alligator's eyes and nostrils stick up just enough to be above the surface of the water.

Alligators can hear underwater.

No matter how slow or
lazy an alligator looks,
it can spring into action
with surprising speed.

Alligators can run very fast
for short distances.

They can slide quickly
down mud banks.

And alligators can climb over things...

...even one another.

Normally alligators do not attack humans, but they have been known to do so. Alligators must kill to eat. A large hungry alligator will grab any living thing that looks like prey...even you! In wildlife refuges, where alligators roam freely, stay near an adult. Whenever you are in alligator country, be watchful near water. If you spot an alligator in the wild, do not approach it. Remember how fast an alligator can move if it wants to.

Alligators play an important role in the wetlands where they live. By dredging up muck and vegetation to build their large, mound-shaped nests, alligators keep waterways clear. This also creates deep holes that hold water for wildlife, even in the driest times of the year. In the moist debris of abandoned alligator nests, new plants grow, and insects thrive.

Wherever there are alligators,
there is sure to be a rich variety of life.